What am I doing here?

Search for self

Grupo Anjos de Luz ®

What am I doing here?

Search for self

Series: Messages of Light to your day

Volume 2

1st Edition

Belo Horizonte
Grupo Anjos de Luz ®
2020

W555

    What am I doing here? - Search for self / Kaká Andrade, Karina Veloso, Maria Alice Capanema, Rita Pereira, Valdir Barbosa (Channelers). Belo Horizonte: Grupo Anjos de Luz, 2020.
    45p. - (Messages of Light to your day ; v.2)

    ISBN 978-65-80152-15-5

    1 Spiritism 2. Psychography 3. Parapsychology 4. Occultism I. Andrade, Kaká II. Veloso, Karina III. Capanema, Maria Alice IV. Pereira, Rita V. Barbosa, Valdir. Title VI. Series.

CDD 133.9
CDU 133.7

Summary

Introduction and acknowledgments

The spiritual evolution goes through each being's energetic purification upon self-knowledge, attitudes and thoughts in the light of Divine Wisdom!

This way, energies may be consciously directed to your protection and to social and personal transformations in order to ascend and ally with the Divine Supreme Energy, God, upon the daily exercise of essential virtues to human being, such as love and forgiveness, peace and mercy, to heal the soul and body, in total harmony with the Universe.

The second volume of the Series **Messages of Light to your day** clarifies you the <u>What am I doing here?</u> on Planet Earth, so that it encourages you to constantly seek the comprehension of yourself and the practice of Jesus Christ's lessons on **the Way, the Truth and the Life**.

The <u>Awakening of the consciousness</u> on <u>I Am</u>, started with the reading of the first volume, is fertile field so that spiritual self-knowledge leads you to a smoother **Walk**, and thus the **Divine Truth** becomes part of you and all matter around you, allowing you to have a fulfilling life.

The messages of this book are directly related to those contained in the first volume of the Series and, when understood, they shall enable the searching and the finding of yourself, of your Pure Divine Essence, and you shall walk in the light to acquire total consciousness in perfect harmony with the Divine Justice.

In this manual, there are instructions to daily exercise of the Virtues and negative energies removal. You will find teachings on the Rays of Light and their vibrant colors, as well as their respective Ascended Masters (Chohans/Directors), who govern the energies of Planet Earth and of all beings who dwell in it.

We thank all Light Spirituality that generously sent us valuable information to a real light meeting!

It is really good to see you again in this search for learning and love!

Introduction

"What am I doing here?"
Search for self

The purpose of this book is to sparkle in you, who is in an earthly experience, the need to raise your virtues and positive vibrations, attracting more of the same Energy of Good and freeing the moorings that hinder your evolutionary walk, so that you succeed at practicing your I Am Divine with mildness.

The path to take during the meeting with yourself is facilitated by widening your Will to live immersed in light, which can be reached with commitment, faith, strength and attention to the instructions being transmitted by the Highest Light Spirituality.

Keep an eye out for your omissions, actions and thoughts, praying and watching always, so that you can figure out what you are doing in this Planet and how to proceed regeneratively, adjusting to the Purest Divine Energy of the Universe, God!

To do this, you will need to protect yourself and daily practice the virtues left by the Father Creator, balancing yourself and creating positive energies through actions, thoughts and feelings aware of and based on Divine Truths.

This way, you shall seek peace and inner harmony, generating necessary healing to carve out a blessed and harmonious life with yourself, with nature and with social and family environments.

Self-knowledge and daily practicing of loving attitudes promote energy balances, revealed since the time of Buddha, and have been widely added to the current practice of medicine.

The findings and scientific and technological advances through research done by scientists on Planet Earth for several years have been incorporating techniques that already exist (Acupuncture, Aromatherapy, Crystal Therapy, Chromotherapy, Flower Remedy, Homeopathy, Massotherapy, Ayurvedic Medicine, Meditation, Shiatsu, Reiki, Tai Chi Chuan, Yoga, among others), bringing new light so that medicine may be performed in search for human wellbeing as a whole (physical, spiritual, mental and emotional bodies), in perfect and vibrational harmony.

We invite you to seek and find yourself in this liberating and welcoming consciousness of the Purest Divine Essence.

Rays, Ascended Masters and Archangels

Light Spirituality of the Great White Brotherhood is formed by Ascended Masters of each Ray (Chohans and Directors of Rays), besides other active Ascended Masters on Planet Earth, along with their Divine Complements, Archangels, Angels, Elohims, Cherubs and respective Light Spirit Workers and Laborers Teams.

All of them act in favor of humanity and devote themselves to the Rays of Lights and Energies that form the bodies of beings and matters, with intensified irradiation of a Ray of Celestial color each day of the week that helps on the maximization of the Virtues evidenced on this day.

We currently have two Instructors of the World: Master Jesus (Joshua or Jesus Christ) and Master Kuthumi. Together, they are the current Coordinators of the works of the Great White Brotherhood on Planet Earth.

There are seven Rays, colors and Ascended Masters (Chohans/Directors/Lords) of the Great White Brotherhood evidenced in this book, one for each day of the week, indicating that you invoke the vibrant Rays on the day of the week, letting you call the ones related to the other days to help you whenever necessary.

1st Blue Light Ray

Vibrant on Sunday, Ascended Master El Morya, Archangel Michael, maximize the Virtues: Strength, Personal Power, Divine Will Protection, Leadership, Faith.

In difficult and discouraging times, imagine yourself protected by the blue color. The blue energy allows restoring faith, strength and balance, providing courage to resume the walk in the search for self.

Decree: Archangel Michael, may prevail in me the Divine Will.

2nd Yellow Light Ray

Vibrant on Monday, Ascended Master Confucius, Archangel Jophiel, maximize the Virtues: Illumination, Science, Knowledge, Wisdom, Technology, Inspiration.

Strengthening yourself in the Yellow Ray and reflecting on the essence of the messages brought by the masters of this Ray will enable the connection to the

Creator in search for Wisdom and Illumination to thread the Path of Light and reach the spiritual evolution.

Decree: Archangel Jophiel, push me to the wisdom of believing in me, in my power and in my light.

3rd Pink Light Ray

Vibrant on Tuesday, Ascended Master Rowena, Archangel Chamuel, maximize the Virtues: Forgiveness, Unconditional Love, Tolerance, Beauty, Goodness, Gratitude.

When humanity understands the power and strength of unconditional love, gratitude and forgiveness will be divine food to soul and light to spirit. Breathe, vibrate and feel love in everything you do in your walk! Be Pure Unconditional Love!

Decree: Archangel Chamuel, may I develop the full and complete capacity for love.

4th White-Crystal Light Ray

Vibrant on Wednesday, Ascended Master Seraphis Bey, Archangel Gabriel, maximize the Virtues: Purification, Karma Cleansing, Ascension, Balance, Purity, Peace, Silence, Resurrection.

The White-Crystal Ray purity allows you to look with joy to the world and everything around you, making the walk full of charms, lightness, and love, charity and achievements learning.

Decree: **Archangel Gabriel, unleash in me the purification of my being towards ascension.**

5th Green Light Ray

Vibrant on Thursday, Ascended Master Hilarion, Archangel Raphael, maximize the Virtues: Healing, Divine Justice, Divine Truth, Concentration, Consecration, Dedication, Prosperity.

Being in tune with the green color vibration will let the gifts of healing, love, humility, charity and forgiveness be exercised and strengthened.

Good and equality will prevail, and all beings will be healed. Peace and abundance will walk together, and everyone will understand they will be united in the Love of Christ.

Decree: Archangel Raphael, release me from judgment, pride and selfishness and may the truth prevail in me.

6th Golden Ruby Light Ray

Vibrant on Friday, Ascended Master Nada, Archangel Uriel, maximize the Virtues: Devotion, Mercy, Love, Healing.

Vibrating in the energy of the Golden Ruby color allows the power, strength and courage to spring in the hearts, illuminating and awakening the souls to fulfill their purpose of love, having only the Creator's recognition.

Decree: Archangel Uriel, give me faith and constancy in prayers.

7th Violet Light Ray

Vibrant on Saturday, Ascended Master Saint Germain, Archangel Zadkiel, maximize the Virtues: Plea, Compassion, Transmutation, Transformation, Freedom.

The Violet Ray invocation facilitates the awakening of humanity to the Divine Truth of transformation and transmutation of all impure and unwanted feelings. Free from dense energies of guilt, rage, regret and sorrow, human being will become aware of their spiritual power derived from pure Divine Love that dwells within each one.

Decree: Archangel Zadkiel, help me transmute my karmas, so that I may reach the liberation and ability to fly towards the Divine.

Among other lights, there is still the Orange Light, a Ray that maximizes the vital energy of the body and spirit all the time and all days of the week, as well as other color Rays that are being presented to humanity in this Earth evolutionary period.

The use of an object or garment of the specified color on the day of the week corresponding to the vibrant Ray is indicated. Your concentration and faith on this day of the week, directed, will expand your own light, facilitating the connection (link to the I Am Divine, God) between your energy and the intensified Light Ray, removing all restrictions.

By tuning with the color vibration of each RAY, the connection to the MASTERS are established, and it will be possible to feel the power of the DIVINE pulsing in you, emanating the CHRISTED LIGHT in all your being.

Initial message

Yellow Ray

Day of the Week: Monday

Virtues: Wisdom, Illumination, Science, Technology, Knowledge, Inspiration
Master Shao Lin Yung: Softness and Lightness
Leader of the Golden Valley Colony

"The Path is unique and lonely.
Each one makes it by himself or for himself.
One who walks clingy chooses the rocky road. But if you
choose to walk gracefully and lightly, your path will be *la vie en rose*: gentle and
scented.
I Am Master Shao Lin Yung."

(Channeled message on 09/24/2018)

Messages from Instructors of the World

Master Kuthumi: Serenity and Trust

"My brothers and sisters in light!

I am here to bring you a word of trust in everything you have been seeking through reading these heaps of messages and all others that have been disseminated daily in your known and unknown social environment!

I ask my brothers and sisters to concentrate and critically analyze the groups you are involved and the readings and videos you have access to.

A selection will be necessary by all of you on everything that comes to you, since the divine Truth dissemination has been expanding in an extremely fast way, just as it is happening with the structural-energetic changes on Planet Earth, which encompasses all the beings, human or not, incarnated or in the spiritual realm.

This expansion is necessary, but it is important it reaches the interested people in their private perceptions and in the level of openness they show to the innovative information that have been passed.

If each one of you do not make the right choice, the opposite effect may happen, the Being's estrangement to the available truths, strictly due to excess that dominates your mind, blocks you and naturally starts repelling the information and, along with it, the divine energies that should enter in your mind and in your daily life!

Therefore, my brothers and sisters, choose with ease the strands of teaching you want to better understand now and, gradually, go deeper into the taught lessons without scattering with information you neither are nor feel capable of understanding.

Be assured that soon you will be ready to leap one more step and continue in the divine ascertainment of your consciousness, to the awakening of your mind and your behaviors in the context of the New Age!

Do not get anxious, because everything will be revealed according to each one's openness, without sudden violations of what you already knew, but with nice and deep transformations in your consciousness, that will take you to true and pure connection to the divine Universe, which is God!

Serenity, my brothers and sisters, is the foundation of divine wisdom!

Take a deep breath, release the dense energy accumulated day by day in you or next to you... breathe once more and imagine the Yellow Ray of wisdom coming down from the top of the head, covering all of your brain and then coming down to your body. Stay in this light for a few seconds and then ask all spirituality of Master Confucius' and Archangel Jophiel's Celestial phalanges to bring you the necessary light to your decision-making!

Afterwards, trust the answers that will be transmitted to you, my brothers and sisters! Trust!

These answers may be identified as a constant thought of what to do, what to choose and how to do, combined with a beating in your heart and a certainty, with little possibility of assurance, but that brings you a feeling of safety, tranquility and relief.

These feelings, combined with the divine teachings, give rise to the certainty of the right decision, in the Path of Light!

Once more, I invite you to trust your intuitions, as this moment of Earth evolutionary change they are powered to a better connection to the Divine!

Many call these intuitions the listening of your heart, because in your heart, the heart chakra, there is the Threefold Flame that was planted in humans by God, so they could expand it and ascend spiritually an energetically.

Intuitions are encompassed by the Pink Ray of pure unconditional love in the divine Truth of good and emotional and material healing, as well as by the Blue Ray of protection and faith in belief in your I Am God, in his pure and divine constitution.

Between these two Rays, in the center, there is the Yellow Ray of Divine Wisdom, that, protected by the Blue Ray and embraced by the Pink Ray of love, has the power of bringing you all the answers to keep your fears and anxieties away and bring you safety that you walk in the Path, the Truth and the Life in Christ, connected to the highest and purest spirituality of good and positive energies of love and peace!

I have been the guardian of Yellow Ray, but I took on the role of coordinating the Earth evolutionary works, along with Jesus. Therefore, my brothers and sisters, I will be here to help you whenever you need it.

You may access my energy in different ways, by invoking me as I currently show you, and also by Saint Francis of Assisi's Prayer, that was intended to me for many Christian beliefs during one of my passages on Planet Earth, and surely before the role of awakening to the Divine Wisdom previously taken by me, which reveals the way to become better and more spiritually evolved each day.

In fact, it is an orientation, so you follow the Path of Light increasing, each daily achievement of the added verses in the Prayer, your proximity to the Greater Energy.

Thereby, my beloved, be instrument of peace of God and sow love where there is hatred. With your attitudes, transmit joy and faith to the suffering or lost in sorrows and doubts, so the divine certainty trespasses them. Console more, comprehend more, forgive more, dedicate yourselves more to others and do not expect anything in return by humans, being aware that the right return will come from the Divine, who will make feasible a happier earthly and spiritual living for you!

Dear brothers and sisters, how wonderful it is to have the opportunity to tell you all this!

In fact, I feel the time has come to all of us unite in ONLY ONE God of love and mercy, in only one Supreme Energy, which soon will be reached through the appropriate and responsible expansion of your I Am Divine of the Threefold Flame inside of you!

I am watching over you every second, along with all laborers and the support spiritual colonies to Planet Earth.

Plenty of Light, my brothers and sisters, of all colors and plenty of Yellow Ray so you reach the Divine Wisdom of what I intended to give you today!

I Am the love and the light in each one of you!

I love you!

I Am Master Kuthumi."

(Channeled message on 07/04/2018)

Master Jesus: Divine Truth

"To my brothers and sisters, have a good morning, a good afternoon, a good evening and a good night every day of your earthly lives!

You should always search for the inner peace in your hearts, letting it be in contact with your I Am Christic, which is GOD, to get the necessary elixir to a balanced, happy and divine life, without stumbling, distressing, angering or hating, without ego restrictions, my brothers and sisters!

These restrictions human being imposes on the spiritual being every day cause sense of loss, emptiness, arrogance, pride, vanities, that provoke in you deep sadness in times of loneliness and confuse your minds, leading to mental imbalances, depressions, strangenesses with your own beings, making many no longer wish to live.

Be aware and watch out, my brothers and sisters, that I love so much!

Have compassion for yourselves and transmute your lives!

Change today your path if something does not please you; however, for this, search for the Path of Light and Divine Truth, that you are GOD, the Power and the Glory for ever!

Illuminated, the right choices will be clear, and you will be able to get rid of the moorings that hold you to the uncared-for ego.

Brothers and sisters, the Truth is that there are not restrictions to the spiritual body, to the power of positive mind in accomplishing your Christian and pure desires without malevolence. There are not, my brothers and sisters!

If you wish to have something that may bring you goodness and help with your evolutions, simply concentrate your thoughts so the energy of the Universe (God) brings the accomplishment to you, which will be involved in the pure Divine Love!

These accomplishments do not have limits either, my brothers and sisters. They may be of any kind — intellectual, personal, material, also financial — as long as they are meant to your good and the others' around you!

Concentration may be done by meditation, prayers, positive thoughts for a few minutes without interruptions and so many other ways of searching for the energy balance.

The recipe for success of your pure desires is given, in the Divine Truth, in the Path that I tried to show you when I was on Earth.

All I did, when I was still human, was to concentrate myself with divine purpose to materialize my healing desires my neighbors and to try to pass the divine message assigned to me.

There is a Threefold Flame of Forgiveness, Wisdom and Unconditional Love inside of you to represent the God I Am in each one of you, as we were all made in the image and likeness of God. The Flame must be kept enkindled, so you do not lose the meaning of life, the incarnations on Earth and the spiritual evolution need.

That is it, my brothers and sisters!

Truth at all times of your day and night!

Truth, peace and love to follow in the Path of revelation that was given you today and has been passed daily through these messengers of light!

Peace and love!

I love you and I am with you,

I Am Master Jesus."

(Channeled message on 04/25/2018)

Messages from Ascended Masters of Rays of Light

1st Ray: Blue Ray

Ascended Master: El Morya
Archangel: Michael
Day of the Week: Sunday
Virtues: Strength, Personal Power, Divine Will, Protection, Leadership, Faith

1st Ray DeCree: Blue Ray
Archangel Michael, may prevail in me the Divine Will.

Master El Morya: Faith and Courage

"Brothers and sisters, be strong! Carry on!

Love will protect you!

The Blue Ray will be around you whenever you invoke it! It creates a true protector shield all over your body and mind. Even in life things will get better!

However, you should be persistent, because everything seems to get worse, to be intensified and may even frighten you in the beginning, but if you have Faith, there will not be room for fear!

Faith wards off fear! They are incompatible!

Faith in God, Father of the Universe!

You forget the Law of Attraction all the time, don't you? So, watch yourselves! Pray!

The concentrated prayer is a meditation that attracts good energies and necessary lights to your protection!

Positive energy attracts more positive energy!

There is negative energy around and do not connect to it. This is only up to you!

If you are not well, pray and receive energy!

If you are well, give energy! Give it to others and search for it to yourself simultaneously!

Let yourselves be supported! Why do you not let it often?

Do you think it is nonsense or you do not deserve it, or you should first redeem from the sins to deserve goodness, forgiveness and world positive energy? No, my brothers and sisters! No!

You can start your self-cleaning right now with prayers and receivings

of energies and, when you are prepared, you give them as well!

God be with you!

Praise your work!

Spirituality thanks you and truly wishes you clean yourselves to meet yourselves.

I Am Master El Morya."

(Channeled message on 07/24/2017)

2nd Ray: Yellow Ray

Ascended Master: Confucius
Archangel: Jophiel
Day of the Week: Monday
Virtues: Illumination, Science, Knowledge, Wisdom, Technology, Inspiration.

2nd Ray DeCree: Yellow Ray

Archangel Jophiel, push me to the wisdom of believing in me, in my power and in my light.

Master Confucius: Threefold Flame

"Light, my brothers and sisters! Plenty of light in your way!

The New Age will be formed by beings full of light; therefore, you need to stay always in the light!

The Yellow Ray brings divine wisdom to your decisions when it is invoked, my brothers and sisters!

It is time you decide for the path of good! So, when you face a state of doubt about what to do, close your eyes and call the Yellow Ray, and you will be assisted by the guardian spirituality of such divine light that will comfort your hearts in the right choices you make! But, my brothers and sisters, trust when you receive the divine message that, in fact, will emerge from your hearts, from the Threefold Flame that is in each one of you.

In Threefold Flame, there are the Blue Ray of protection and faith that vibrates to your right, the Yellow Ray of divine wisdom to the center and the Pink Ray of unconditional love and forgiveness vibrating to your left, forming the divine spark left by God Father in each human being incarnated on Planet Earth. This Flame remains alive, but, for many, very incipient and frosted. Do not leave it this way, my brothers and sisters! Keep it slightly alive every day, and you will be protected and will not leave the path of light!

The Yellow Ray will bring you a constant thought about what should be done, dispelling doubts.

But if you still do not have so much faith to believe in your inner voice, add your thought to the practical effects that will be produced and, if good, mercy, forgiveness and charity prevail, you can be sure you will be covered by the light in your decision. Believe!

Wisdom is in every act, in every step taken based on all divine teachings that have been transmitted to you! It attracts success in all fields of your life because it is closely related to positive thinking that produces energy and attracts more positive energy.

Plenty of Yellow Ray to all brothers and sisters every day!

Be at peace with your consciences!

I Am Master Confucius."

(Channeled message on 05/09/2018)

Master Lanto: Wisdom and Balance

"Wisdom, my brothers and sisters, in love teachings, is recognizing all of you are constantly learning on Planet Earth or spiritually out of it!

All social organization you are in today is a result of a millenarian evolution, with merit to the inhabitants of Earth to the highest technologies access and to Medicine, Physics, Chemistry and Biology discoveries, among so many other sciences that have been ascertained every day.

The Truth is that holistic sciences came to us due to the evolutionary level all earthly beings are in, so they remain at the same evolution pace of the Planet itself, as they need to comprehend that all medical-technological evolution happen under the light of Divine Wisdom too, sent to those who connect to it, combined with elevation to the conscious level that everything and all evolutions are followed by the gradual raise of each one's I Am Light divine consciousness.

Science, technology and faith in divinity of pure energy of the Universe have always gone together, my brothers and sisters! But few had cognitive and conscious access to them. It did not mind to many because they believed themselves and in the power they had themselves, and thus they ended up connecting to the Supreme Energy, attracting to themselves, with the power of their thought and the belief in their hearts, the Yellow Ray of Wisdom that helped them to follow in their experiments and reasoning, until they reached important conclusions and beneficial innovations to health and life as a whole to humans and other beings incarnated on Earth, from animals to plants and vegetables in general.

But now it is time for us to join this knowledge, my brothers and sisters: Science and Faith! Every discovery, even the ones that have been transmitted in spiritual level, involves the energetic essence at its core, moved by its own energy, and because of that it was discovered the atom and its function, which is pure energy to form all matter on Planet Earth.

This energy joins others forming substances and so on, producing more energy around it.

Therefore, be aware that everyone, being energy, produces energy as well, either by their movements or by the power of their thought, even stronger when the thought comes from their heart beating!

Brothers and sisters, it is exactly because of this I ask everyone to watch their feelings, as all kind of intensified energy produces more of the same energy, including the bad and dense ones. For this reason too, we are constantly bringing everyone the awareness that you should purify your thoughts and energy every day, so you connect just to good energies, attracting the Sublime energy of peace and love to you, enabling the pure contact with golden energy of Divine Wisdom to guide you with safety in your spiritual and earth walk!

You may channel your energies to achieve all your personal, professional, financial and family successful purposes, my brothers and sisters!

But, this attempt will only be reached to good if you are connected to positive energies, so that you have enough strength to remain or reestablish the connection to the divine spirituality and guardian of your virtues, warding you off all the evil and restrictions, if anything negative disturbs you or takes you out of the way.

Feel you deserve this knowledge and many others that have been transmitted and make good use of them! Practice them!

Finally, I would like to warn you to be careful with your emotions!

When you cry out for your hearts, it means your I Am Divine that is in your heart chakra, this perfect and pure I Am, that was not sullied yet by greed, vanity, lust, fear, insecurity, anxiety and by many other restricted and dense energies.

The I Am is in your heart and, connecting the human to the Pure Divine Energy of the Universe, you may hear all the answers to your questions clearly.

But for this, you need to have faith in all of this and in yourselves too, not a blind faith, but a rational faith ousted from exaggerated emotions that unbalance your energies!

It may seem strange, but an unemotional faith is strengthened by directing your thoughts to what in fact is good to you and others around you, and because this faith/belief is linked to something rationalized, to a positive purpose, it will bring you the same energy of good, without uncontrolled emotions, clearly!

Meditate! Pray!

May your hear pulse in the divine light and all of you may access your voice that emerges from your I Am Divine, left by God the Father in each one, so the raise of consciousness attracts the Yellow Ray of Divine Wisdom to humans and you may be gifted with more peaceful and bright discoveries every day, for a better life on Earth and in spirituality!

I Am Master Lanto, who assists in the balance of those who wish to stabilize their emotions and access their inner I Am!"

(Channeled message on 07/11/2018)

3rd Ray: Pink Ray
Ascended Master: Rowena
Archangel: Chamuel
Day of the Week: Tuesday
Virtues: Forgiveness, Unconditional Love, Tolerance, Beauty, Goodness, Gratitude.

3rd Ray Decree: Pink Ray
Archangel Chamuel, may I develop the full and complete capacity for love.

Master Rowena: Divine Forgiveness

"My brothers and sisters!

Be persistent in the divine light of Unconditional Pure Love!

This light that irradiates in the world, bringing a strong charity in your hearts through compassion by your mistakes and by others' assistance!

Be patient and kind to yourselves! Forgive yourselves!

The daily mistakes may perfectly be tackled with honest regret and with behavioral change of your routine.

For this, be vigilant and watch closely your behaviors with yourselves and others around you, especially your family, besides friends and coworkers.

Love can be exercised through an understanding look at inappropriate and devoid actions of spiritual and energetic logic from those who are still lost and unbalanced of the beloved Heavenly God's divine and pure light!

So, have compassion!

And if you realize that you also unbalanced yourselves and acted untimely, unlike what is expected in the positive energy connection, calm down and forgive yourselves!

Invoke the lights and your guardian angels, as well as all Light Spirituality that insists on assisting you in this phase transition on Planet Earth, and they will come to you!

The free will, used in the purest love, will be the solution for your problems in the world!

Regretting at things done wrong and changing the course of your way is something wonderful, bringing lots of joy to the spirituality that takes care of you! It is not lack of merit; on the contrary, it is pure merit of spiritual evolution in this incarnation!

Love unites you! Hatred, contempt, distress and rage divide you and scatter the positive energy necessary to your protection in this mix of dense energies on Earth!

Be strong in faith and do not scatter yourselves!

This is the New Age that is coming, that needs a previous energetic cleaning on the Planet, and, for this, many energies are confused, drawing on religious teachings to evil, in total lack of nexus and logic. At the end, this energy explosion will serve to separate the good ones from the bad ones; therefore, protect and prepare yourselves to the New Age of good and love!

Everything will settle down and each one's evolutionary process that remains in the earthly plan will be more evident, less painful, and the divine forgiveness will fall on those who deserve it, who request it with the purest and most honest love, with purpose of a true spiritual and behavioral change in incarnation.

May the Pink Ray of unconditional love, forgiveness and goodness embrace you now and forever, bringing a happier day and a moment of inner regeneration for each being!

I love you so much!

Invoke the God I Am, which is the divine energy that is in your hearts, with the Pink Ray of Love!

I Am Master Rowena of the Pink Ray of unconditional love."

(Channeled message on 06/20/2017)

Master Rowena: Love and Peace

"I am a being of the Pink Ray of unconditional love, who came here today to transmit to all of you the feeling inherent in love and forgiveness, in peace that forgiveness brings!

Love and forgiveness: the recipe to a proper spiritual evolution to each incarnate light being!

Do not connect yourself to bad energies! Forgive yourself when you lose the divine teachings: do it all the time!

Forgive the others and endeavor for it. You will succeed!

This will set you free from incarnation ills in human body, that are marked by other past lives!

Be aware, always!

So be it!

I Am Master Rowena."

(Channeled message on 04/27/2017)

4th Ray: White-crystal Ray

Ascended Master: Seraphis Bey
Archangel: Gabriel
Day of the Week: Wednesday
Virtues: Purification, Karma Cleansing, Ascension, Balance, Purity, Peace, Silence, Resurrection.

4th Ray Decree: White-crystal Ray

Archangel Gabriel, unleash in me the purification of my being towards ascension.

Master Seraphis Bey: Faith and Courage

"My brothers and sisters in light!

I bring you a message of light for your day today and for you to take it for all the other days!

I know that many times the problems seem so difficult that they cause discouragement to the raise of faith planted in your hearts.

But be sure the strengthening of this faith, with the warming of your heart, may face them healthy so you rise again stronger in spirituality and in divine pure love.

Listen to your hearts, that is, listen to those messages transmitted to you by spirituality on how to act in faith!

Observe, though, the listening in the rationalized faith, devoid of exaggerated emotions that turn your comprehension blurred, avoiding the erroneous path decision of the self-watering and all the confusing feelings it, when in evidence, causes in human being.

All humans are spirits of light in evolution, corrupted one day by prisons caused by self-overvaluation, such as vanity, feeling of superiority, narcissism, prejudice of all kinds, as you were the most correct and perfect beings, even causing humiliation, discouragement, despising others, without admitting your own mistakes, your own flaws, still under evolutionary treatment.

But, brothers and sisters, these times of self-prevalence, to cause fears, frustrations, insecurities, are passing by and it is important that all of you enter in the divine energy in search for perfection.

Think with all the strength and faith that you are perfect, so you attract more spiritual perfection. Always link your thoughts to isonomy and equality of the earthly beings, so you do not despise anyone and do not act as you are better than anyone else, but with a self-assessment you feel better as persons and spirits in the divine teachings, to serve as an example of love and charity to those who seek someone to mirror in order to evolve.

The search for perfection, my brothers and sisters, firstly goes through the forgiveness of the past in other incarnations and experiences in this current life.

It also goes through the practice of unconditional love, that may be reached by forgiveness, mercy and charity, such love that should be spoken and shown, my brothers and sisters!

In order to reach it, search for the connection to the divine energies that are in you!

Search for the peace and balance among body, mind and spirit!

Everyone needs calmness in this fast-paced earthly life.

The calmness of the mind, especially in times of great difficulty, will bring light and divine connection so you understand what you should do get rid of the problems in a health and evolutionary way.

It is this peace of mind, my brothers and sisters, that will make you listen to the messages of your heart correctly, without emotional interferences caused by the ego, becoming your guide of rationalized faith to lead your steps towards the spiritual perfection and the spiritual evolution, ascending your yearnings to materialize your pure desires!

Be at Peace! Search for peace!

Peace! Peace! Peace!

Plenty of White-crystal Ray!

I Am Master Seraphis Bey."

(Channeled message on 05/23/2018)

Master Seraphis Bey: Joy and Peace

"Yes! Say yes to love and joy!

Let the joy enter in your life as a flame that warms your hearts, because everything in life is easier when there is joy and love!

Smile! Love!

Forgive yourselves! The true forgiveness of others makes us happy and it attracts more fullness and opens the paths to your redemption!

It has already been said that without charity there is no salvation!

Everyone who does or has done charity work knows how much joy arises in our heart and Saint-Christi-Being!

The peace is quiet and calm, and the joy becomes peaceful to all confrontations!

Happiness is not only in small things, but also in great things! It is a pure and peaceful state of mind!

May the peace and purity of the Holy-Spirit-of-God I Am be renewed in each one and transmit the peace of Christ to the world!

Believe in each learning. Put it into practice and you shall be happy!

May the White-crystal Ray pacify the incarnate and disincarnate beings!

Plenty of peace,

I Am Master Seraphis Bey."

(Channeled message on 03/30/2017)

5th Ray: Green Ray

Ascended Master: Hilarion
Archangel: Raphael
Day of the Week: Thursday
Virtues: Healing, Divine Justice, Divine Truth, Concentration, Consecration, Dedication, Prosperity.

5th Ray Decree: Green Ray

Archangel Raphael, release me from judgment, pride and selfishness and may the truth prevail in me.

Master Hilarion: Balance and Harmony

"May the Green Ray of healing be with all of you!

In this earthly race, the daily challenges try to bring you down, besides the physical weariness, and it is necessary to take care of the key thing: the Spiritual side.

Battles are fought to balance all senses of the earthly life, joining the physical and spiritual senses. The physical supports the daily earth basis, and it should be fed and taken care so there will be a perfect harmony with the performance of your functions.

The spiritual is fed by your thoughts, joy, love, so it may give support to the physical body and together they interact in perfect synchronization.

When they are not aligned, there are imbalances, the illnesses originating and reflecting in flesh body (physical). Keep the spirit harmonized in order not to jeopardize the other and vice versa (physical and spiritual).

Brothers and sisters, the great secret of this earthly life is balancing both bodies (physical and spiritual) and continuing in this evolution defined since your reincarnation. Be aware of how to treat your physical body through earthly medicine, medication, vitamins, exercises and how to take care of yourselves healthy so you may fully manage the outlined missions.

These challenges are big, ennobling your earthly development.

Taking care of the spirit through prayers, meditations, positive energy flows that are fed spiritually, putting your Coronary Chakra (located at the top of the head, responsible for linking the being to God, the Pure Divine Essence) in perfect balance, free from stains or erasures, is the purpose that I and the Father have for all of you, my brothers and sisters.

Observing one part or another, have yourself balance, take a rest, meet yourself, meditate and you will find your balance point.

Healing comes from yourselves, brothers and sisters, from your faith, remember that the Master mentioned in his passage on Earth: faith moves mountains. If your faith is like a mustard seed, you will tell the mount to move to another place and it will obey you.

Strengthen your faith, my Brothers and Sisters, never miss it, however difficult the battle may be. The Father does not abandon his children. Nurtured, you will be safe and firm in the mission as discussed before.

I leave with all of you this Green Ray, balsamic upon your family, and the Universe, so the burden becomes softer and lighter as a feather. Brothers and sisters, I am very grateful for leaving simple and short messages, so you do not forget them on a daily basis. Although all of you know your duties, the messages should be always dictated!

I love you all, my Brothers and Sisters.

I Am Master Hilarion."

(Channeled message on 10/23/2018)

Master Maria: Balance and Respect

"Dear children!

Sometimes I am appalled by so much distress you have been going through on Planet Earth at this moment!

But also, I quite often try to understand why it is so difficult for people to follow the path of Jesus Christ?

I know the evils caused by self-elevation and, hence, the inadequate practice of your choices, out of your proposed free-will, have allowed too dense energies to weigh on you during the centuries, and still weigh on many until today. These energies are gathering themselves, my children, and you need to be careful, so they do not affect you.

The similar energies, for the spiritual/energetic world of lights, end up attracting each other, they do not repel each other.

So, my dear, you should understand that many of them are gathering themselves improperly in several places of the Planet, because they are being repelled by energies of light that are expanding to the karmic change of the Planet they live in now, which will select less dense and more illuminated energies to remain in it.

Children, I respectfully ask you and touch your hearts during this reading, I AM begging you now, to open your hearts for the entry of God the Father, that is, for the positive energies brought by the Supreme Universe of love and mercy!

That will be necessary, so you protect yourselves from bad energies around! They gather themselves to similar ones and end up taking beyond people with full conditions of remaining in the light, who did nothing, exactly because these people did not give their spirit, or for many, their soul, the proper attention and necessary care!

You do not take care of the spirit with material behaviors, my dear! It needs good energies, evolutionary learnings, charity practices, mercy, self-forgiveness, forgiveness of others, unconditional love to the neighbor, which includes even the respect to your executioners!

Children, wake up! Rise!

Start now resuming your spiritual path, because, without it, there will be big chances you succumb to evil energies around! I know for thousands of years that there have been diversities of interpretations about God and the several doctrines and dogmas, even with criminal behaviors of many people, which happen until today. However, it is time to squirm out of these concepts tied down to both past and present, ousted from the divine teachings.

For this, I advise my dear children to read or study the Gospel of Jesus without considering many interpretations! The cold-reading of the texts from the Bible may bring you back to the Christian course. Surely if you already have any dogmatic/

doctrinaire belief, you may make your own interpretations, you may adjust speeches said by Jesus at that time to present time. This may happen as long as you never conclude with exaggeration or extremism what you extract from the reading, especially if your conclusions lead you to a feeling of repulsion to other religions and non-extremist dogmas.

Children, all good religions and doctrines lead to a unique place: God!

It does not matter the classifications used for each one or the path that the spirit will follow after the physical body death if the important thing is, at least in this moment of energetic transformation of the Earth, that you evolve your spirit in this life through your Christian ethics and behaviors!

This plea at this moment surely does not deplete itself in this speech, as there is spiritual life after disincarnating.

But, for many, speaking about it is a taboo; so, I just ask these people who do not wish to step into this knowledge now that they simply understand it will be here, in this earthly life, the most important moment for your spirit to survive well and faithful to God, who is inside your soul, covers your body and gives life to it!

You need to act in divine mercy now, dear children!

I have communicated all my concern with you here today, because I have been seeing losses of wonderful people, who had been working on their commitments made in free will, but due to negligence, they have ended up losing themselves to madness, to illnesses of physical body, and even to self-flagellation and death!

In recent weeks, I have received many prayers and energies from faithful Christians and from other unfaithful ones, but who deeply and honestly pray, and I tell you that I LOVE YOU VERY MUCH and I deeply wish you have spiritual health, because only like this you will achieve the full happiness and love, as they (fullness and love) are inside of you and will expand with your own transformation!

Watch and pray always, my dear children!

May My blue cloak, along with the Celestial phalange of Archangel Michael's soldiers, protect you from all negative energy and may the Green Ray of Divine Truth trespass your mind and your heart in order to bring strength and healing to your minds and bodies, in energetic and spiritual balance and harmony!

With all my great and infinite love, we will be next to you and will always answer the sincere calls to your daily resurrections to the Divine!

I love you!

I Am Master Maria, Mother of Jesus and all of you!"

(Channeled message on 08/22/2018)

6th Ray: Golden Ruby Ray

Ascended Masters: Nada
Archangel: Uriel
Day of the Week: Friday
Virtues: Devotion, Mercy, Love, Healing.

Master Nada: Goodness and Mercy

"My Children!

My intention today is to dedicate a word of Mercy to all brothers and sisters on Earth!

This word consists of the information that you will have the Divine Mercy with greater readiness during this period of energetic reformulation of the Planet you live in, to comprehend your karmic problems and also the ones created by current experience, due to different choices of the commitment made in free will for your evolutionary process.

This comprehension provides you the power of compassion stronger in each one, in order to enable the true forgiveness for your own mistakes and for all who one day have caused harm to anyone or anything on this Planet, provided by God!

For this, children, it is necessary to give thought to your acts and admit your mistake with honesty!

There is no problem, my brothers and sisters, to make mistakes without Christic consciousness of the harm caused, as long as one day you see the truth that permeates the mistake and its consequences. This truth is directly related to the identification of the mistake to the restrictions brought by the ego, which distorts the I Am Perfect in God who is in each one of you.

These imperfections were evidenced in Jesus Christ's teachings when he passed by this Planet. He tried to show everyone that the mistakes should not prevail, and they can always be fixed with sincere forgiveness and unconditional love. This love was really proven by examples of Jesus' mercy and charity to his brothers and sisters.

But I ask you to give thought to this entire passage of Jesus positively, without guilt or sorrow!

Yes, Jesus suffered as human, but what he actually wanted to transmit was not his eternal suffering, but that there will be suffering in spirit and evolution of the brothers and sisters who insist on making mistakes, especially after having their consciousness raised to the Perfect and Supreme Energy of the Universe.

The intention was still to demonstrate, through behaviors practiced by a human, how you can really practice all virtues of the perfect spiritual being that is in you every day.

It is important that you see a Jesus Christ happy to help people, to have mercy and to practice forgiveness every day, even for the worst evils, as it happened in his crucifixion.

Dear children, Jesus was extremely happy in his passage, especially when He practiced mercy and forgiveness, because this way He was totally free!

Practice forgiveness and set yourselves free, my children!

Set yourselves free from all bad feeling that devastates you!

Forgiveness and unconditional love are the path to your liberation and your happy and light walk!

The biblical passages where Jesus presented sayings in a serious and strict way are important to transmit you that the evolving and following the path of goodness are, in fact, important and serious steps in your life.

They should be connected to the impartial and Supreme Energy without exceeding exaggerated emotions, in order to allow the seemingly cold balance, as in some biblical passages, be the guiding element and strong point to annul both bad and good sentimental exacerbations!

Understand it! You may love unconditionally, but you should have balance to practice this love to others, at the risk of interfering, before improper exaggerations, with your loving neighbor's evolution, besides unbalancing yourselves!

I know this comprehension may seem difficult now, but I tried to explain quite objectively the practice of divine mercy, which involves unconditional love, forgiveness, divine will, charity, among other virtues, all of them practiced in a balanced way, my dear children!

Search for your spiritual and energy balance and try every day the purification of your beings towards the encounter with the I-Am-Perfect-and-Divine rescue, in straight connection to God!

Gradually, reading and reading again all messages that have been sent you, you will have peace of God to keep you from stumbling, aware that you are beautiful and perfect, in constant spiritual growth, towards the Supreme Energy! You may, therefore, relieve your passage on Earth in the light of Divine Mercy, so each day may be happier and fuller!

I love you! I will always be here to touch you and reinvigorate each one's heart with goodness and mercy!

With love,

I Am Master Nada!"

(Channeled message on 08/09/2018)

Master Nada: Charity and Forgiveness

"Mercy, my brothers and sisters!

Today I bring you this message!

A message of pure and divine love for forgiveness and mercy of the soul and body!

When you get upset, whether with yourselves, with others, or with social and natural causes of life, have mercy on you and your neighbor!

Children, siblings, friends, parents and other relatives, as well as strangers and colleagues deserve our mercy, especially because you deserve it yourselves!

Mercy is a mix of love, forgiveness, charity and salvation, my brothers and sisters!

It brings peace and relief to your emerged feelings! It moves rage and hatred away and brings the sense of becoming better and more evolved people!

Just be careful of not becoming snob, since you are neither better nor worse than the others. You may just be in a more advanced evolutionary stage, and thus you may benefit more from the goodness of the world, attracting more goodness and positivity to your earthly lives.

You may suffer less in life, my brothers and sisters!

Believe in the divine power inside of you, in the power of mercy!

Have faith that the practice of mercy, in the simplest and in the most complicated moments of your lives, will bring you resignation and abnegation of all bad feeling that, quite often, devastates your minds and, hence, your physical and emotional bodies.

Have mercy on your disaffection – it knows not what it does – but you will know how to forgive him and have mercy on him, so that you follow your lives without moorings and free to pure love and purification of your spiritual and carnal beings.

In mercy, nothing is expected in return! Just the full practice of goodness is felt, just it!

May our Heavenly God have mercy on all of us and you on Earth, the mercy of love and forgiveness to happy, liberating and full life!

I love you!

Jesus loves you and is with you!

I Am Master Nada of Golden Ruby Ray, power of strength of love, faith and mercy."

(Channeled message on 11/04/2018)

7th Ray: Violet Ray

Ascended Master: Saint Germain
Archangel: Zadkiel
Day of the Week: Saturday
Virtues: Plea, Compassion, Transmutation, Transformation, Freedom.

7th Ray Decree: Violet Ray

Archangel Zadkiel, help me transmute my karmas, so that I may reach the liberation and
ability to fly towards the Divine

Master Saint Germain: Transformation and Transmutation

"It is time to transform, my brothers and sisters!

It is time to awake to the divine truth!

There is something far beyond what humanity, in its majority, so far understood about what they are and where they are in all the planetary systematic context!

Humans are just one of the species that lives the worldwide orbit, considering as world the comprehension of everything they reach in earthly thought.

Several species existed on Planet Earth and human being is one of them. Planet Earth is the place to live for different kinds of beings, materialized or not.

We all make part of a unique Universal system, led by Supreme Greater Energy, pure and divine, whose revelations will be transmitted gradually, so a New Age may be healthy established on Planet Earth.

These revelations pass by the discovery of each one's spiritual value.

Self-knowledge, within the perspective on existence of a pure and divine light-spiritual being inside each inhabitant on Earth, will open the doors of greater knowledge that will be transmitted. In fact, they are already being transmitted at all times.

Only with the expansion of divine consciousness in each one you may reach more knowledge and connect yourselves to the pure energies of the Universe, to keep you in harmony with new evolutionary energies that will hover over Planet Earth.

Those who do not succeed in connecting to this knowledge will end up losing themselves energetically to dense energies and will be addressed to other Habitations, so they can connect to the evolutionary energy of New Age through free will.

There is always time, my brothers and sisters!

It does not matter what you did in past lives or in this life, in this special moment!

Divine mercy will be granted to all lost ones, even the worst of beings, so you have a chance to transmute your vital energy and change as before.

By forgiving yourselves and the others, involved in pure unconditional love, you may regenerate yourselves and connect to good energies!

Believe! The Father Almighty, Universe of goodness and love, will give you the opportunity to be better people and spirits from now on!

Ask for divine protection, so the Celestial phalange of Master El Morya, assisted by Archangel Michael and all Light Spirituality designed to the beings' protection within the Faith, covers you with a pure energy of the Blue Ray, forming a bubble around you! Call for an increase in faith, powered by this Sparkling Blue Ray. Use the Blue color a lot, my brothers and sisters!

Faith! Plenty of Faith!

With the power of your thoughts, invoke the color and the Yellow Ray of divine wisdom, so they give you the necessary intuition to good and transformed use of your free will.

The Pink Ray of unconditional love will be expanded by forgiveness and will bring a sense of mercy, even to the self, when it is involved. This mercy, that comes from the power of Faith inside each one,

may be powered by the Golden Ruby Ray that, for a long time, has been taken care of and sent by Jesus, the Christ your earthly consciousness knows. In amplitude, it will be known that today Jesus acts strongly as Coordinator of all of us in the works on Planet Earth, and Master Nada as Chohan/Director of this Ray.

My brothers and sisters, the transparent White-crystal Ray will make you ascend all your purest and most divine desires, showing humans that your earthly life can be better, as long as you are connected with the Highest energies.

When the White-crystal Green Light is invoked, it helps healing, along with the Blue Ray of Mother Mary's holy cloak, Our Lady Mother of Jesus on Earth, who protects and helps all her children in self-healing, healing others and developing technologies in medicine to heal, along with Master Hilarion.

When the Violet Flame is invoked, my children, it cleans all the environment, cleans the being of all evils of the ego and prepares the transmutation of your being to divine raise.

I am guardian of this Ray of Light, which is more evident in these 2 thousand years, with the 2000s in this energetic spectrum of consciousness transformation of the beings, as they are involved in the mission of regeneration on Earth and in the energetic evolution of the beings, incarnated or not.

My children, the Orange-Crystal Light is subtle and brings the necessary vitality to your recovery when you connect to dense energies and feel extremely absorbed and tired.

Do not be lulled by low energies around you!

The Orange Light protects from depressions that take even to self-extermination.

It protects from self-flagellation behaviors and other beings' flagellation, as it inebriates the being with vital energy, which is, by its essence, divine.

Understand your children and protect them from all evil!

Pray a lot to attract these protective and transforming energies!

Read spiritual messages, biblical ones, when you are focused on a full happiness in God, with the Universe! Keep yourselves away from dense energies!

Today, the reading is easily accessible, with social network and device technology, highly developed for this evolutionary moment and dissemination of divine truths. Therefore, do not use them to disseminate any evil or self-evidence associated with fear, insecurity, evil, among many other bad energetic vibrations!

I love you all and I will be here working constantly in spirituality and directly with human beings, in order to enable to those who believe in the truth of the Pure Divine Energy to transform their lives and follow the path of light and good!

I Am Saint Germain, who was on Earth as Saint Joseph, husband of Mary and father of Jesus Christ, and who has the mission of assisting in transmuting the Planet Earth and all beings that live in it!

I Am the Violet Ray in each being!

Hallelujah! Hallelujah!

I Am Master Saint Germain."

(Channeled message on 06/26/2018)

Final Messages of Divine Wisdom

Master Jheriel: Love and Peace

"Hail Mother Mary and all Angels of the Blue Ray!

The Planet needs all to send Blue Ray to all beings. The Blue will allow a pure and balanced connection among the distressed and disturbed minds. The Blue of

Mary's Cloak will make all beings unite in a sole purpose: balance, love, peace and serenity.

All beings – minerals, plants, animals and humans – may and should find peace. Each realm, in its level of evolution, needs balance to become more and more conscious of its role in the evolution process on Planet Earth.

Love very much! Love for your life and for the life of all beings. Be the beings that are in the micro-organisms stage, even the humans that are still in complete darkness – everyone, without exception, need love.

The Blue color will allow your hardened minds and souls to open so the Pink vibrating color takes care of the beings in all levels of spiritual evolution. The Pink vibration of love will irradiate from every beings' hearts and from the entire galaxy.

I bless you all with the Blue Ray so each being emanates the vibration of the Pink color, the color of unconditional love.

In times of despair, fear, weariness and discouragement, inhale the Blue color and feel yourselves supported by Our Mother Mary's Cloak!

With peace, love and gratitude.

I Am Master Jheriel."

(Channeled message on 07/12/2018)

Golden Ruby Ray
Virtues: Mercy, Devotion, Love, Healing

Chico Xavier: Abnegation and Dedication

"My brothers and sisters in Christ!

Be your own guide to lead your path in Jesus' teachings, to your earth and spiritual evolution, as this moment Planet Earth has also been going through an energetic change and a change to the disincarnate and incarnate spirits that live in it. These spirits, still lost, but with the energy of love emanated by those who understand the need to be forwarded, may also be served and follow the path of light!

I am a friend of yours who remains in spirituality to assist you, especially the brothers and sisters who live in Brazil, as I have dedicated to spiritual works close to needy people for a long time, also transmitting the example of love and dedication to the neighbor, as a mission entrusted to me by Light Spirituality.

Emmanuel, who guided me a lot, along with André Luiz and many other Light Laborers spirits, helped me in this process and they still act effectively, each in its own way, on behalf of emanation of the divine teachings to all who truly wish to evolve.

Some of them already reincarnated and others still in light try to transmit love,

34

charity and practice of good every day, as means to our salvation, as I remain in this energy of love, still in other dimension, which soon many of you will reach in connection too, even though alive in the flesh.

Dear brothers and sisters, read more on the spiritist doctrine, the books I have written in connection to the Light Spirituality that sent the messages, so you may know more and more how the spiritual side works, and, with it, you have sympathy and connect yourselves healthy, avoiding bad consequences of disengaged behaviors from Christ's teachings.

However, first and foremost, if you succeed in reaching the spiritual connection, the energy inputs will be already open in your etheric beings, which will prepare the energetic field to deeply assimilate the blessings the energies of lights of all colors bring to each spiritual being, forming connections between other divine beings, incarnate or not, in a great chain of protective light to help you overcome all problems that will arise from this moment of changes and confused and tumultuous energies.

This is very important, my brothers and sisters! Connect yourselves to the divine energies!

I am here in spirituality, often going to Colonies of medical-spiritual treatments and welcoming people without spiritual belief as an incarnate being, but who see in me a source of trust and recognition as a medium on Earth.

I tell you this so you may follow the same path of abnegation and dedication to your neighbor, in the spectrum of the personal and professional earthly mission you assumed in incarnating, in order to disseminate Jesus Christ's teachings through love and charity and transmit the truth to your neighbor, related to the belief of spiritual life existence after death.

The Workers who assist needy people in body and soul healing should pay close attention to do volunteer work, without any self-evidence, but should be happy for being expanders of examples that each living earthly being's I Am has healing power and harmony, as long as in healthy connection to Light Spirituality!

You gain faith of the unbelievers with it!

Yes, my brothers and sisters, keep acting as an example to your neighbor and take it to your private life, so there you may also act as an example of love and charity experiences!

Finally, I wish you a good path, resignation in the virtues powered by lights of all colors and the certainty that it will make a difference for you and for the other who comes to you!

The Orange Light refers to vitality and think of it whenever you feel absorbed energetically. Then, invoke the other divine lights in the colors of virtues you wish to emphasize, especially the blue of protection. Therefore, you will be able to raise whenever you are temporarily dejected by dense energies or obsessor spirits that approach you!

I now say goodbye, informing you that I am around, seeing each one's battle who has read this simple message and telling you this fight has not been in vain. On the contrary, it will bring better fruit in spiritual life, and now, with the evolution of Planet Earth, it will also bring a better life to those who live in it and understand the importance of the connection to the Supreme divine and perfect energy, which is God!

I love you!

God be with you and may our Lord Jesus Christ continue in the command, keeping you from all evil!

I Am Chico Xavier."

(Channeled message on 06/06/2018)

Yellow Ray
Leader of the Golden Valley Colony

Master Jheriel: Illumination

"Hail Our Lord Jesus Christ and Virgin Mother Mary!

I am really happy to be here in this very special moment.

Moment of reconnection to the Divine, where all beings are striving to search for the light and understand the mission to perform on Planet Earth.

Many people think that fulfilling the mission is just helping others and do charity. It is much more than this.

Performing the mission is illuminating yourself to illuminate the Planet.

And how do you illuminate yourself?

It is necessary to quieten the mind, to listen to the soul and to feel the life flow with the heart. It is to understand how magic this existence is. It is to connect to the Universe! It is to connect to the cool breeze of the morning. It is to illuminate and bathe yourself with sunbeams while walking to the west. It is to allow the birdsong to fondle your mind. It is to feel the perfume of the plants invading your spirit. It is to understand the look of an animal asking help and to be able to feel its pain, its fear, its affection and above all its gratitude.

Is it simple? Sometimes it is not, because ego tries to live in people's soul. Do not feel ashamed at undressing the vanity and be simple.

Take care of your soul with love as you take care of your body. Feel yourself beautiful to life! Let life flow and operate miracles in your walk. Make of your walk a moment of lightness. Transform the stones into steps to reach the highest point of your journey: ILLUMINATION!

Always vibrate the rainbow colors, and when you go to sleep, cover yourself with Our Mother Mary's Blue Cloak and feel protected, sheltered and strengthened to start a new dawn of faith, light and hope.

With peace, love and gratitude!

I Am Master Jheriel."

(Channeled message on 07/19/2018)

Green Ray
Advisor Ismael — Member of the Medical-Spiritual Team of Great Heart of Astheriãn.

Advisor Ismael: Amendments are not Sonnets

"It is not possible to reach the peak without going through the ascent of the mountain.

Many people ignore the need of respecting the steps in life and want to go too far without subject knowledge.

And they get lost in the way... they do not evolve... they retroact.

And a tremendous pain stays in the heart.

Nobody wants to return, nobody wants to fail, and it is not necessary to let this happen, as long as we know how to go with life flow, step by step, calmly, rhythmically, peacefully as someone who knows what they do and where they want to be.

Everything conceives in a rhythm in life, in its own life time.

Who governs all this?

The divine experience, our centerline.

There is no way to extrapolate the basic things in life without losing ourselves in the way.

The stages are necessary, they are growths that allow us to see how great and perfect the mystery of life is.

Let us learn, then, to fulfill our journey step by step, without rushing to reach, but with plenty of coherence in each step made.

God protects us, but He does not guide us without our own steps.

He grants us the right to contribute to our own journey.

Let us halt our disoriented rhythms and let us search for the peace and joy of conquering a safe and constant path that reserves us the right to dream and edify.

I Am Ismael."

(Channeled message on 02/27/2013)

Message from the Leader of the Medical-Spiritual Team of Great Heart and Astheriã and Grupo Anjos de Luz

Green Ray, Blue Ray, Yellow Ray and White-crystal Ray: Dr. Helmuth - Member of Evolutionary and Helpers Council

Dr. Helmuth: The Path to Soul

"May the name of Christ be praised!

Hail the Medical-Spiritual Team of Great Heart of Astheriã.!

As I mentioned in Book 1 <u>Who AM I? - The awakening of the consciousness</u>, this Book 2 <u>What am I doing here? - Search for self</u>, we will start together the great Search. Search that will show how to conquer and climb up the steps of the evolutionary scale. Searching is a learning of love, self-knowledge, forgiveness, responsibility, discipline, commitment, humility, overcoming, with yourself at first and extended to family, friends, neighbors and all those who will help you to find yourself and to find out at the bottom of your soul, your spirit, the Greater Essence of Pure Divine Love of the Father, The Master of Masters, the Architect of Universe, God.

The encounter with yourself is continuous and gradual. This comprehension of who **I Am** and **What I am doing here** is the beginning of a great journey of soul in search for its pure essence, of the awakening of collective consciousness, understanding, comprehension and acceptance that everything is good for you, it will be good for your family, your neighbor, your street, your community, your district, your city, your country, to Planet Earth.

The awakening of Unconditional Love is nothing more than loving yourself, seeing yourself without disguises, appreciating the virtues you have, working hard to change your misbehavior to life, to your family and to your neighbor. It is to remember that all change starts with yourself, in your thoughts, feelings and behaviors, anyway, that charity starts in your house. Honor your ancestors, love, honor and look after your parents, love and educate your children, remembering that it is not enough to love your children, it is necessary to set limits, love and limits always walk together.

And finally you will be able to see in your neighbor your own reflection, because the Unconditional Love shows all your beauty, magnitude and wealth. It is Light that never ends, it is Light that illuminates even more, it is Light that overflows in all beings of Planet Earth, directing the course of incarnation journeys in search for evolution, understanding and comprehension of awakening of collective consciousness.

The journey of soul will be guided by Unconditional Love that shines like Divine Light in each one. In the 7 Rays of Lights, Ascended Masters, Archangels and Decrees presented in this Book, there is an alchemy, a universal panacea able to heal all diseases that torment the human being. The effective medication is the Unconditional Love.

The 7 Cosmic Rays are the Greatest manifestation of Divine Love and are concentrated in executing the Plan of God to the Planet Earth and the Universe. In the first Ray, you will find the pure manifestation of Divine Will. In the second Ray, you will silence your mind to listen to the Divine Voice. In the third Ray, your will release your soul from negative energies, that is possible only through the Unconditional Love, taking you to full consciousness that on Earth we are all brothers, sisters and children of the same Father, God, awakening, thus, the feeling of Fraternity. In the fourth Ray, you will understand the feeling of Unit, you will learn how to work on behalf of Integration and Purification of humanity in perfect harmony. In the fifth Ray, you will learn how to appreciate even more the Plant Kingdom, as source for encountering the Pure Divine Essence of Healing. In the sixth Ray, you will understand the true meaning of Abnegation, Detachment, Devotion, Mercy to the Assistance free from interests to everyone who needs you. In the seventh Ray, you will feel how important guilt liberation is to your Purification and Transmutation, opening yourself to receive the Divine Mercy.

I especially thank the Medical-Spiritual Team, which I have the opportunity to lead, guide, coordinate and learn, and I have learned with these dedicated spirits united in light, goodness, collective consciousness of unconditional love, great love that guides, directs, makes all obstacles be overcome one by one.

My immeasurable recognition to the Workers and Laborers Team specialized in Supporting from-distance or in-person medical-spiritual treatments. These illuminated spirits committed to healing provide tranquility, safety, balance, vibrational harmony in all continents of this Planet where we are performing.

Gratitude to the Mediums Team that volunteers to the spiritual attendances, since in those days they involve for countless times their hearts in the transformed and transmuted light of the Threefold Flame, setting themselves at service of love, light and good.

Gratitude to the Helpers Team (Friend Angels) that are always available to contribute with work, readiness, knowledge.

Finally, each one gives the best inside the heart: LOVE. And we cannot by love, we cannot sell it, we cannot put a price on it. LOVE is simply demonstrated in thoughts, feelings and attitudes.

I thank you Father of Mercy and Infinite Love, Jesus Christ, Virgin Mary, Christ, Patron of Planet Earth, for all the gathered blessings in all days of work, and may we continue along the way of light and learning, humility, discipline, forgiveness, comprehension, acceptance, patience, tolerance, compassion and mercy, winning the difficulties and tribulations.

In this current Age of Aquarius, Planet Earth will benefit from the expansion of collective consciousness, that will direct and strengthen life of all humanity. And I insist again, may all of you learn to forgive, comprehend and accept yourselves and the other as they are, to be merciful, to be compassionate, to work without complaining, to do good unto others, to study continuously without laziness, to be punctual, assiduous, committed, responsible and, mainly, do not forget that all good, peace, light, love and abundance you unceasingly implore to heaven is right in front of you.

Search and you will find, knock and the door shall be opened, and with your soul's light you will find what you are looking for. New lives, new Times, Unconditional Love and Teamwork define everything.

Praised be Christ!

Hail the Medical-Spiritual Team of Great Heart of Astheriãn..

I Am Dr. Helmuth."

(Channeled messages on 03/25/2018 and 11/17/2018)

Inspiring Prayers

Invocation to Archangel Michael

Archangel Michael in front of me,
Archangel Michael behind me,
Archangel Michael on my right side,
Archangel Michael on my left side,
Archangel Michael over my head,

Archangel Michael in my heart,
Archangel Michael beneath my feet,
May He guide me to all the good paths
And wherever I go
The blue light from His sword
Bless me, protect me, guard me, support me
But deliver us from all the evil
Today, tomorrow and for all lasting days of my life.
Amen, amen, amen, amen!

(Source: www.grupoanjosdeluz.org.br)

Prayer of Saint Francis of Assisi

Lord make me an instrument of Your peace.
Where there is hatred let me sow love.
Where there is injury, pardon.
Where there is discord, unity.
Where there is doubt, faith.
Where there is error, truth.
Where there is despair, hope.
Where there is sadness, joy.
Where there is darkness, light.
O Divine Master grant that I may:
not so much seek to be consoled as to console;
to be understood as to understand;
To be loved as to love;
For it is in giving that we receive;
It is in pardoning that we are pardoned;
And it is in dying that we are born to eternal life.

(Source: www.grupoanjosdeluz.org.br)

Forgiveness, Love and Gratitude Mantra of Grupo Anjos de Luz

Today I forgive myself.
And I forgive all at this moment.
I apologize.
I am sorry.
I love myself.
I love all.
I am grateful.

I am free!
All are free!
So it is.
So shall it be.
It is done!
Amen, amen, amen, and amen.

(Synthesis of Ho'oponopono arranged by Grupo Anjos de Luz)

Ho'oponopono is a process for us to dissolve toxic energies that exist in us in order to enable the impact of thoughts, words, achievements and Divine actions[1].

Other prayers on the website www.grupoanjosdeluz.org.br

Decrees

Decree is like a prayer, a wish, an instrument and a way of meditation that guides us to work, develop and strengthen the virtues we need to our spiritual and improvement growth.

How to do it:
Procure um lugar tranquilo e sente-se confortavelmente em uma cadeira, com a coluna ereta, ou se preferir, em posição de lótus, caso não seja possível, deite-se e relaxe.

Respire suavemente: inspire pelo nariz e conte até três, expire pela boca contando até três. Repita a sequência quantas vezes julgar necessário, até sentir-se relaxado. Faça o exercício com tranquilidade para que sua mente se esvazie de todos os pensamentos. Mas, se surgirem pensamentos, não se preocupe, mande-os embora.

Pense, mentalize na cor do Raio referente ao Decree escolhido, padrões

---

[1] VITALE, Loe; LEN, Ihaleaka Hew. Limite Zero: o sistema havaiano secreto para prosperidade, saúde, paz e mais ainda. Rio de Janeiro: Rocco, 2009.

(atitudes) que necessita trabalhar, ser amparado(a) ou desenvolver.

Repita o Decree três vezes e em seguida agradeça.

Se preferir, faça diariamente, meditando o Decree referente ao Raio do dia e se possível faça também a leitura de uma mensagem referente ao Mestre.

Desta forma, você poderá conectar-se com mais profundidade na essência de cada Raio e absorver com mais clareza os ensinamentos dos Mestres Ascensionados e Arcanjos.

Orai e vigiai sempre!

Luz, paz e bem!

1st Blue Light Ray Decree

Archangel Michael, may prevail in me the Divine Will.

Day of the Week: Sunday

Virtues: Strength, Personal Power, Divine Will, Protection, Leadership, Faith.

Archangel Michael speaks of human will delivery to Divine Will.

2nd Yellow Light Ray Decree

Archangel Jophiel, push me to the wisdom of believing in me, in my power and in my light.

Day of the Week: Monday

Virtues: Illumination, Science, Knowledge, Wisdom, Technology, Inspiration.

Archangel Jophiel provides contact with Divine Wisdom.

3rd Pink Light Ray Decree

Archangel Chamuel, may I develop the full and complete capacity for love.

Day of the Week: Tuesday

Virtues: Forgiveness, Unconditional Love, Tolerance, Beauty, Goodness, Gratitude.

Archangel Chamuel helps with love awakening.

4ᵗʰ White-crystal Light Ray

Archangel Gabriel, unleash in me the purification of my being towards ascension.

Day of the Week: Wednesday

Virtues: Purification, Karma Cleansing, Ascension, Balance, Purity, Peace, Silence, Resurrection.

Archangel Gabriel guides the flame of ascension and the karma burning.

5ᵗʰ Green Light Ray Decree

Archangel Raphael, release me from judgment, pride and selfishness and may the truth prevail in me.

Day of the Week: Thursday

Virtues: Healing, Divine Justice, Divine Truth, Concentration, Consecration, Dedication, Prosperity.

Archangel Raphael provides cleansing and stripping to receive the truth.

6ᵗʰ Golden Ruby Light Ray Decree

Archangel Uriel, give me faith and constancy in prayers.

Day of the Week: Friday

Virtues: Devotion, Mercy, Love, Healing.

Archangel Uriel awakes the compassion and mercy.

7ᵗʰ Violet Light Ray Decree

Archangel Zadkiel, help me transmute my karmas, so that I may reach the liberation and ability to fly towards the Divine.

Day of the Week: Saturday

Virtues: Plea, Compassion, Transmutation, Transformation, Freedom.

Archangel Zadkiel not only brings transformation, but also life organization to be free.

Final message

"Dear friend,

We wish you that, finding Who **I Am**, your heart may be light and happy, ready to take the Path of Soul understanding and accepting the **What I am doing here** and fulfill your mission on Planet Earth with Love for self, for everything and for everyone around you.

Medical-Spiritual Team of Great Heart of Astheriãn..

Pray and watch, always!
Light, peace and goodness!"

(Channeled message on 11/18/2018)

Gratitude!

More information at www.grupoanjosdeluz.org.br